Moose Live Here

Moose Live Here

BY IRMENGARDE EBERLE

Doubleday & Company, Inc., Garden City, New York

BOOKS BY IRMENGARDE EBERLE

PICTURE CREDITS

Cover photograph by Jack White from National Audubon Society.
Allan D. Cruickshank from National Audubon Society, pp. 6, 25, 28, 41.
John H. Gerard from National Audubon Society, p. 31.
Hugh M. Halliday from National Audubon Society, p. 54.
G. C. Kelley from National Audubon Society, p. 46.
Ben McCall from Annan Photo Features, pp. 22, 32.
McIntyre from Annan Photo Features, p. 16.
Karl H. Maslowsky from National Audubon Society, pp. 37, 57.
L. David Mech, p. 52.
Charles J. Ott from National Audubon Society, pp. 13, 19, 45, 51.
Leonard Lee Rue from Annan Photo Features, pp. 14, 35.
Leonard Lee Rue National Audubon Society, p. 20.
W. J. Schoonmaker from National Audubon Society, pp. 26, 58.
Jeanne White from National Audubon Society, pp. 11, 38.
Joe Van Wormer from National Audubon Society, p. 48.
Colin Wyatt from National Audubon Society, p. 42.

Library of Congress Catalogue Card Number 72-105682
Printed in the United States of America
First Edition

To Phyllis Grossman

The long, cold winter with its sub-zero weather was over. Spring had come over Alaska and Canada's Yukon Territory.

The great bull moose, browsing on budding broad-leafed plants beside a small river at the border of the two countries, was comfortable at this season. Only a few months ago he had carried six-foot antlers on his head. But in midwinter they had fallen off and the new ones he had grown since were not very large yet. They were not a great burden to him.

As he ate he raised his head and saw his mate some distance away. But he kept on feeding, for she was of no importance to him now.

The cow moose was more alert and restless than he today. She and the bull were huge creatures. Even in early summer, when they did not have their full weight back after the lean months of winter feeding, she weighed over 1600 pounds. Her mate was heavier and larger, and both of them would put on more pounds during the summer months. He would soon weigh 1800 pounds. Moose are the largest animals of the deer family.

Along the stream's bank where they browsed, there was a flat strip of land, overgrown with willows, poplar, and other trees. The new leaf buds and twigs were good eating for moose. The cow kept feeding steadily. The bull came up close behind her. She did not want him near her at this season, so she grunted roughly at him and left.

Finding herself a new place, the cow rested and chewed her cud. The stillness of the wilderness was unbroken except for the chirp and twitter of birds and the soft swish of an otter coming up out of the water where it had caught a fish. The cow seemed content, yet even now there was a vague urge in her to move on.

She became fully aware what this urge meant. Her calf would soon be born. She arose and started to walk. She must find a hiding place for herself and the coming young one. It must be a place where there was little chance that any of the large wild animals would find and endanger her baby. Not even her mate, or any other fellow moose, must be nearby.

Toward the west lay a lake. She walked steadily toward it. Reaching its shore, she looked across to a small wooded island lying in the still water a hundred feet or so away. The island—that was the place she chose. She walked into the lake and began to swim with mighty strokes of her strong legs.

About a mile out in the water she saw another moose cow. Moose are great swimmers, and this one was probably headed for the far shore. The first cow saw only that this moose was not going her way. That was good.

She kept on swimming toward the island. Reaching land, she let the water run off her back and soon began to browse again. After some hours she found herself a good hiding place among bushes and young trees. There her calf was born.

He lay on the ground, helpless and weak, and so much smaller than she. She would take care of him with all her strong moose motherhood instinct. She stood close beside him watching him intently, touching him softly with her big, rubbery nose now and then. But she did not urge him to get up. He must gain strength first.

After a while she lay down beside him and let him suckle. Her milk nourished him and strengthened him. When his hunger was satisfied he lay still, dozing. His mother arose and stood—watchful and alert. In another half hour she nudged him more firmly than before. She was urging him to try to arise now. He struggled several times and failed. At last, gathering all his strength, he got up on his weak, wobbly legs, and stood beside her. This was important. A young wild creature must, for safety's sake, get control of his body as soon as possible.

The nights were getting shorter at this season of the year here in the far north country, and the days longer. But the darkness still could be depended on for a long time to help the mother hide the young one. She stayed with him hour after hour.

At last she grew hungry and thirsty. The calf was lying down, sleeping again. She nudged him and gave low grunts, as though telling him what to do. Then she left him for a little while. He seemed to know that he must stay in this place surrounded by thickets, and did not try to follow her. He lay with his thin, big-jointed legs spradled out, his great, dark eyes wide open, and waited for her.

The cow did not go far away. Down at the lake, which lay still and flat in the pale sunlight of the oncoming northern evening, she drank. Then she browsed hungrily on young willows and poplar leaves. She took the branches in her mouth, pulled them through her thick rubbery lips and strong teeth, tearing the leaf buds and small twigs from them. Then with her jaws full, she chewed. And all the while she kept her senses alert so she would know if danger came near her calf.

In about two hours she was ready to go back to him. She looked around her, sniffed the air. No bear or wolf seemed to be nearby, so none would see where she went. Quietly, she stepped into her secret place.

As she approached her young one, she grunted again, and he answered her with high, crying sounds. In another moment they were together.

The young one grew stronger each day, and with increasing strength he became a little bolder. On the third day he followed his mother out of the hiding place and stayed near her while she ate. She wandered quite far from the young one's birthplace now, but she always did her browsing near thick bushes, so that the calf could run in among them quickly and hide, should danger come. Always the cow moose sniffed the air at short intervals to catch the scent of timber wolves on the breeze if such should come near. But there were few on the island—that was why she had come here. Whenever she did get such a scent, she pushed her calf with her nose and grunted at him. Then he quickly darted into a thicket and hid. At other times, when they were out in the open, he grew tired of watching her feed and went back into the brush of his own accord, to hide, rest or sleep a while.

There came a time when the cow moose had the urge to go back eastward to the mainland from where she had come. One day, with the calf close beside her, she stepped into the shallow water and waded forward. Her young one followed, caught up with her and stayed beside her. The water grew deeper as they waded onward, and now the cow began to swim. This was new to the little one, but he tried it too. He did pretty well, but it was hard to keep up with his big, strong mother. He lagged, and she stopped and waited for him. He laid his head on her back so that she could support him the rest of the way. Then they went on.

When they reached the shore the cow moose quickly led her calf to high grass where he could hide again. While he nestled down out of sight, she looked about her, then, as usual, began to feed. Moose eat about thirty to fifty pounds of green stuff a day. She ate in the bright sunlight, and in the rain. She ate in the long daytime, and often during the night too. In between she stopped, lay down somewhere, and chewed her cud.

The food supply had grown rich as summer came, for the plant leaves had unfolded and were broad and juicy.

In time the calf began to eat some leaves as his mother did, even though he still suckled. Day by day, they walked farther from their familiar grounds. Before long they were miles away. They seldom met other moose. From a distance they saw a bull, and another time a cow moose with twin calves. Even these the cow moose avoided.

She was always alert, watchful. But in spite of all her care, the calf's life was full of danger. Several wolves had already smelled the young one for some days and knew where he was. They started toward the odor. But because the mother kept too near the calf, they went silently back into the forest again and again.

Then a black bear caught the moose scent too, and came to see if there was a calf he could attack and eat. The wind was from another direction, and the mother moose had not smelled his coming. The calf was a few yards behind her. The bear stopped a little distance away and stared at them, trying to figure out whether the space between mother and calf was wide enough so that he could risk a snap at the calf with his big jaws and strong teeth. But now the cow moose saw and smelled him. Instantly she charged. The bear turned and fled. Big as he was, he would not risk being struck by her hard hoofs. He would wait for a better time to try to get that tender bit of meat. Excitedly the cow went back to her young one, who had hidden himself at her first warning sound. In the thicket she calmed down and lay with the calf.

Usually, even when danger lurked some distance away, the cow and calf did not know it, so most of the days and nights were peaceful for them. The young one ate more and more leaves, and less milk from his mother. Midsummer had come. The nights were now very short and the days long. The calf had grown fast. They both liked water plants that grew in the lake bottom. When they ate these near shore the calf followed his mother and did as she did. When she dove into fourteen feet of water to eat far out at the bottom, he stayed behind.

One day the cow and calf came upon the bull moose who was the young one's father. He had wandered in the same direction as they. He stepped toward them, and the mother moose charged at him as though he were one of her enemies. And he was, at this time, for a bull moose takes no interest in his calf. He has no father instinct. Indeed some have trampled their young to death. So the moose cow guarded against the bull. He saw her rage and, like the bear, left quickly.

The young calf had changed as he grew. But he was still not like a grown moose. His mother was a dull gray-brown, and her hair was coarse. His hair was a more reddish brown and much softer. His ears were longer in proportion to his head, and his eyes were dark and large.

Still more weeks passed, and the calf learned to swim better every day. He was no trouble to his mother now when she swam a long way in a river or lake. Often they saw water birds when they were on their way—birds which had wintered in the south and had flown back to the north in the spring.

The cow and calf came upon flocks of mallard ducks some days. They passed close to them, but moose and ducks did not disturb each other.

Again when the cow and calf were on land, an old danger arose. Two of the timber wolves that had been watching them all along took courage and came quite near. Again they waited for the cow moose to get quite a distance from the young one as she browsed. The wind blew the wolves' odor away from the cow, and she did not know they were nearby.

At last the two timber wolves saw what they wanted. The mother moose, intent on feeding, had allowed herself to go too far ahead of her calf. Swiftly the wolves ran toward the young one. They came lightly, making almost no noise. If they could reach the young one before his mother came back, they could jump at the calf's throat and quickly kill it. Then they would run a short distance away. The mother moose would come to the calf's defense, but it would be too late. Seeing he was dead she would stay awhile and try to make him come alive. But she would see that it was of no use, and after a while she would go away. Then the wolves would come back and tear off the flesh of the calf's body and devour it.

The wolves' mouths watered for the taste of that meat.

They ran faster. Just before they reached the calf, the mother moose turned and saw them. She ran with all her might and got between them and the young one. Her head was lowered and the hairs on her neck bristled. She snorted furiously and lifted her powerful front legs. This was the closest that danger had come to her calf yet.

The wolves stopped and then dashed away. Just like the bear they did not risk being trampled by a big powerful moose. They lost themselves again among the forest trees. They were not so hungry now in summer that they needed to take chances with an aroused moose. There were many smaller animals such as the snowshoe hares, which they could catch and eat with less trouble.

The summer daylight lasted almost the whole twenty-four hours now early in August. Dusk and pale darkness was all there was of the brief nights. The calf was quite big and strong by this time—though of course still much smaller than his mother. He no longer drank her milk but lived entirely by browsing. The cow did not watch him quite so closely any more.

Scattered throughout the forest and bits of open land, the bull moose, old and young, were shedding the fuzzy growth called velvet, which covers their antlers all the first part of the year.

They rubbed their head structures against trees and rocks, as other kinds of deer do, to get rid of the loosening velvet. The soaking that their heads got when they ate water plants helped too. Gradually, all the velvet came off in ragged strips, and the antlers were free of it.

August was the beginning of the mating season too. A great bull moose browsed a half-mile from the cow and her big calf. He sniffed the air and at first did not scent them. He wandered on, and after a while the wind shifted and he caught the scent of a cow. He ran in the direction that his nose told him to go, giving his call. Coming out of the forest into a stretch of flat open land he saw the cow and her half-grown calf and ran to them.

The cow had been restless all that day. The mating instinct had awakened in her again too, and her former mate was not here. She waited for the new bull moose, ready and eager for him to approach her. As he came near her she was not at all unfriendly as she had been with the other bull earlier in the summer. Then it had not been the right season for getting together. Besides, there was no danger to her calf now. He was big and strong, and no bull would harm him.

Bull and cow greeted each other in moose fashion, with sniffs, silences, and an occasional grunt. And after a while they mated. They stayed in the same area for some weeks. A new young moose calf would be born to the cow in about eight months.

The calf kept close to the cow and bull as they fed. He was not giving up his mother, and she did not push him off. Gradually the cow and bull moose began to feed a little farther apart again. And in the coming months the bull became a loner once more, or walked with another bull or two.

It was often still quite warm for a few hours during the brightest part of the days as summer faded. Then the cow and calf would find a shady, damp place and wallow on the ground, and rest there, as they had often done all through the warm season.

When browsing the cow sometimes itched because of insect bites. Then she would scratch her front with a hind leg, or rub her rear against a tree trunk. The bull scratched with his antlers wherever they would reach.

The calf lost his baby coat and gradually grew a new one—still brown in color, but with a grayish-silvery tinge. This new coat, as it slowly came in, in August and September, was quite thick. Nature was beginning to prepare him for the intense cold of the coming winter. The older moose began to shed too, and grow warmer coats.

The antlers of the bulls, throughout the land, were at their full width and height as autumn drew near. Some of the older ones had antler spreads of about six feet; others, according to their age, had three-, four- or five-foot antlers. The yearlings had mere spikes. Every year they grew slightly larger ones. Those of the older moose had spikes and also large, flat, or palmate areas. The large antlers of some moose became very heavy to their wearers. They were also difficult for the bulls to handle as they made their way through forest or brush land. Their heads were provided with thick, strong bones to hold this horny structure, but even that was not enough to make the great growth comfortable to carry.

Already at the beginning of September, food became a little scarce. Many of the leaves turned brown, and were no longer juicy. Besides, there were other animals scattered throughout the forest and the open land, who also fed on the leaves and twigs of bushes and trees. There were a number of other moose, though they were thinly scattered, and there were caribou and other deer browsing. This made food still more scarce.

The cow moose and her calf wandered on and on as they looked for the remaining good leaves to eat. They were now perhaps twenty miles from the place where the calf had been born in the spring. They were in open land, but mountains lay only a few miles away. Sometimes on their wanderings they saw single moose. Now and then they saw a little group of five or six browsing together. But these did not form a real herd, nor did they stay together long.

Cold weather came early here in the north country. One afternoon the first snow flurries whirled about the cow and calf. When it stopped, the ground was only partly covered with white. Soon rivers and lakes froze over. Heavier snowfalls came. The cow and her young one did not mind. Their thick coats and the fat they had grown under their hides in summer kept them warm. Besides, the snow and ice were a natural part of the lives of these northern animals.

They did miss the bountiful food of the summer, however. Now they had to scratch away the snow with their hoofed front legs to find bits of edible plants, such as grass, lichens and roots that could still give them

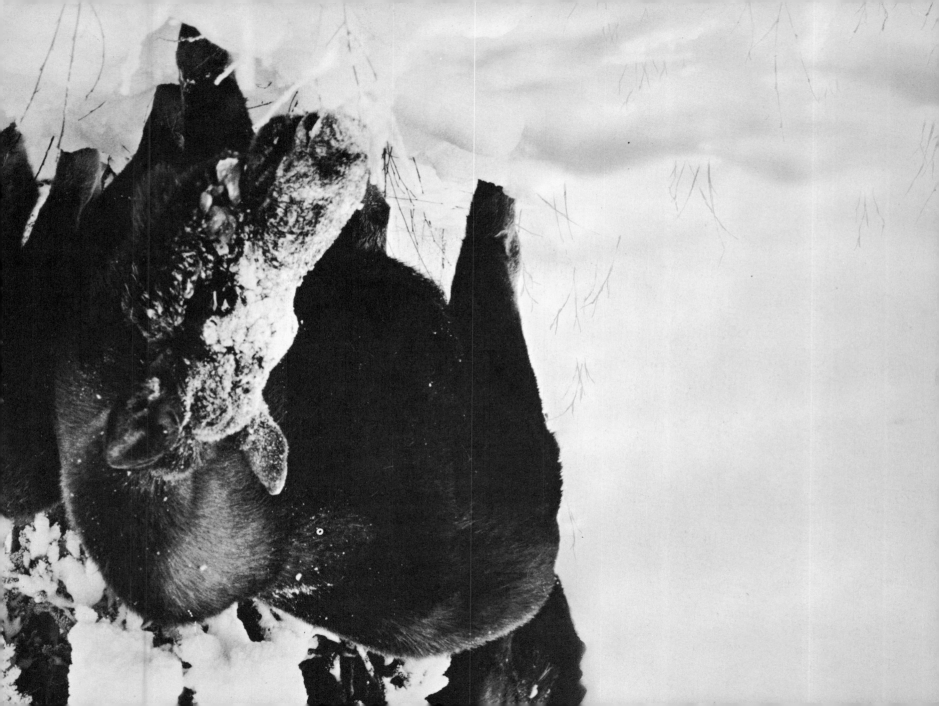

a little nourishment. Working in deep snow their noses came up white as they lifted their heads to chew. They walked knee deep in drifts. They seldom if ever ate the green tips of spruce trees in spring or summer, but now they did.

The hours of darkness grew longer until it was night almost all the time. The few hours of winter sunlight gave almost no warmth at all.

Like the other moose of the north these two often lay down in the snow to rest. Once they passed another moose comfortably lying in the snow. Another time they came upon a cow who had a big calf with her. Now and then they saw lone bulls or cows, or two or three together. But they did not stay long with these rarely seen neighbors.

In some areas five or six moose yarded for a while. They briefly formed a group, trampling the snow and making a sort of yard where they stayed, seeking food by digging up roots and browsing on bark or fir tips all around them. But most moose kept to themselves or went about with one or two others briefly. All were hungrily seeking food.

One day our cow and calf came to a place where there were many timber wolves running in one direction—pausing and then running again. The wolves did not bother the cow moose and calf because they were big, healthy, and strong and could defend themselves too well. They were stalking a very old cow moose who trotted slowly a little way ahead. She was too weak and shaky to fight the wolves.

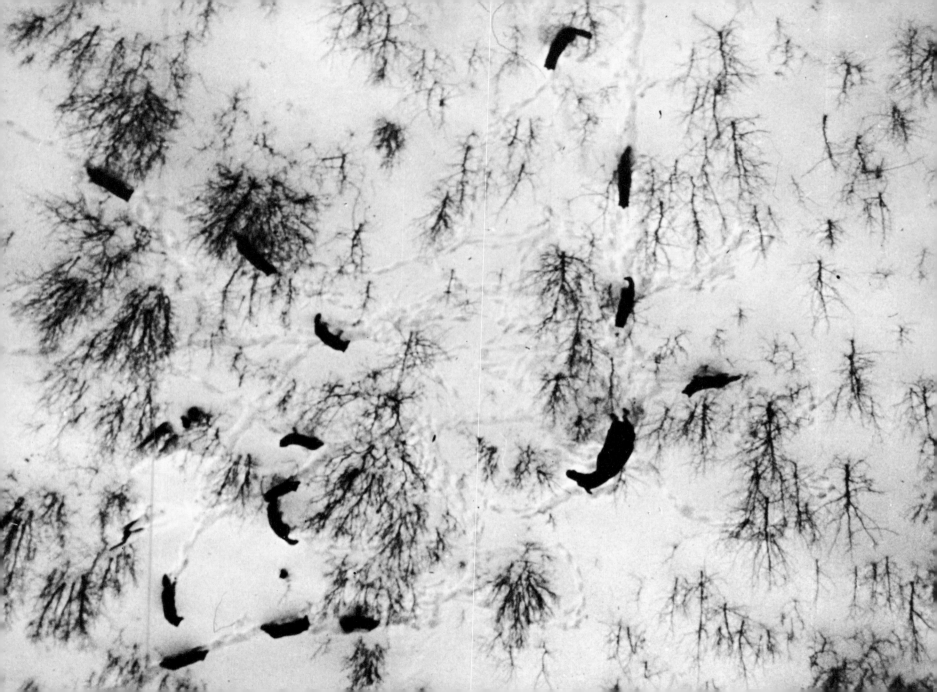

She did keep running, and for a while managed to stay ahead of the wolf pack. But soon she sensed that they were all around her and stopped. Now she looked around her helplessly. The wolves crept closer. One of them jumped at her throat, then another. So they killed her and in a moment all the pack fell upon her and began to tear her flesh and eat.

Our cow moose and her strong young calf had turned away from there quickly and never saw the end. At first they were disturbed for a while because of the presence of the many timber wolves in this area. But as they went farther and farther, and left these behind, they forgot about them. And, as was their moose way, they did not wonder what had happened to the aged cow.

Late in December the older bulls began to shed their magnificent antlers. They were eager to get rid of them, and knocked the big structures against trees and rock outcroppings to help loosen them. The cow and calf came across many of the knocked-off antlers in the snow, and they often saw bulls still working at theirs to shed them. Before long all the older moose had theirs off. Then they looked almost like the cows except for their greater size. But they soon began to start growing new ones. These, during the first months, were small and light of weight, and not awkward to carry.

The younger bulls of various ages dropped their antlers later. Some of this went on all through the months from December through March. The older bulls dropped their antlers early because these needed a longer time to grow their larger antlers back to full width and height by the next August. Some of the younger ones with only smaller spikes did not drop theirs till spring.

All the while there was one snow storm after another, and now the cow moose often walked through snow that reached almost to her belly. There was less and less to eat. Gradually she and her calf grew leaner. They were often close to starvation.

At last, long after spring had already come to places like Washington State, New Hampshire, or New York, milder weather set in here in the Far North too. The ice began to break up in lakes and streams. The snow melted and ran off into the brooks, rivers and lakes. Finally the leaf buds on the trees burst open, and grew green and juicy. The time of plenty had come again!

The hungry moose cow and her calf, which was now a yearling, ate day and night with only short rest periods in between. The wild birds that had flown south in autumn were coming back. They, as well as those who had stayed, were nesting. Again there were ducks and other water fowl everywhere. Bald eagles built their nests high in fir trees.

The yearling moose was quite independent now. He browsed farther and farther away from his mother. Gradually he became entirely separated from her in his wanderings.

That was just as well. For now the moose cow had no time for him anymore. She would soon search for a hiding place again, and give birth to a new young moose in some safe thicket tinged with the pale green of swelling leaf buds.

Irmengarde Eberle has written nearly sixty books for children, and some of them have been published overseas in twenty-seven languages.

She came east from her native Texas shortly after graduation from college to become an editor and a writer of adult articles and fiction. Her keenest interest lies in writing fiction and factual books for the young, particularly the warm portrayal of animals to children in accurate natural history. She collects the illustrations for her wild animal books from the outstanding wild-life photographers of the United States and sometimes of other countries. She has won several awards, and a number of her books were Junior Literary Guild Selections. Five universities have asked to collect her manuscripts and other papers. The main collection is at the University of Oregon.

She served at one time as a reviewer for the New York *Herald Tribune*'s books section. She was also one of the originators of the Children's Books Section of the Author's Guild and for ten years their Children's Book Committee Chairman. She has lectured at Columbia University's writers' workshop and elsewhere.

She and her husband, Arnold W. Koehler, live in New York City.